God Made Me

- from -

A to Z

God Made Me

- from -

A TO Z

26 Activity Devotions
for Curious Little Kids

Allison Key Bemiss

An Imprint of Thomas Nelson

Published in Nashville, Tennessee, by Tommy Nelson. Tommy Nelson is an imprint of Thomas Nelson. Thomas Nelson is a registered trademark of HarperCollins Christian Publishing, Inc.

Tommy Nelson titles may be purchased in bulk for educational, business, fundraising, or sales promotional use. For information, please email SpecialMarkets@ThomasNelson.com.

Unless otherwise noted, Scripture quotations are taken from the International Children's Bible®. Copyright © 1986, 1988, 1999, 2015 by Thomas Nelson. Used by permission. All rights reserved.

Scripture quotations marked NIV are taken from the Holy Bible, New International Version®, NIV®. Copyright © 1973, 1978, 1984, 2011 by Biblica, Inc.® Used by permission of Zondervan. All rights reserved worldwide. www.zondervan.com. The "NIV" and "New International Version" are trademarks registered in the United States Patent and Trademark Office by Biblica, Inc.®

ISBN 978-1-4002-4704-2 (softcover)
ISBN 978-1-4002-4706-6 (eBook)

Written by Allison Key Bemiss

Illustrated by Angelika Scudamore

Library of Congress Cataloging-in-Publication Data

Library of Congress Cataloging-in-Publication Data
Names: Bemiss, Allison, author. | Scudamore, Angelika, illustrator.
Title: God made me from A to Z : 26 activity devotions for curious little kids / Allison Key Bemiss ; [illustrated by Angelika Scudamore].
Description: Nashville, Tennessee, USA : Thomas Nelson, [2024] | Audience: Ages 2-5 | Summary: "Teach preschoolers their ABCs and faith using the hands-on, sensory experiences and projects in this creative activity devotional that explores living for Jesus with curiosity and excitement"-- Provided by publisher.
Identifiers: LCCN 2023042750 (print) | LCCN 2023042751 (ebook) | ISBN 9781400247042 (paperback) | ISBN 9781400247066 (epub)
Subjects: LCSH: Devotional calendars--Juvenile literature. | Christian children--Prayers and devotions--Juvenile literature. | English language--Alphabet--Juvenile literature. | LCGFT: Alphabet books.
Classification: LCC BV4870 .B444 2024 (print) | LCC BV4870 (ebook) | DDC 242/.62--dc23/eng/20231002
LC record available at https://lccn.loc.gov/2023042750
LC ebook record available at https://lccn.loc.gov/2023042751

Printed in India

24 25 26 27 28   REP   10 9 8 7 6 5 4 3 2 1

Mfr: Replika Press / Sonepat, Haryana, India / April 2024 / PO # 12194837

To the little children and their grown-ups who read this devotional, may the time you spend reading and exploring together turn into faithful, fun memories that last a lifetime. You were in our hearts and prayers as we created each page.

Also to my mom, thank you for getting the jumbo crayons when I needed them and for your patience while I used every last bit of color. And to Daniel, my own personal flashlight and anchor on any adventure, and my boys, Elijah and Jonah. Being your mom is my favorite answered prayer. I love you exactly as you are.

—A.K.B

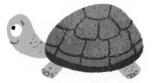

CONTENTS

Note to Families		viii
How to Use This Book		x
☐ **A**:	I Am Adventurous	1
☐ B:	I Am Brave	5
☐ C:	I Am Creative	9
☐ **D**:	I Can Discover	13
☐ E:	I Am Excited	17
☐ F:	I Am Faithful	21
☐ **G**:	I Am Grateful	25
☐ H:	I Am Hopeful	29
☐ **I**:	I Am Inclusive	33
☐ **J**:	I Am Joyful	37
☐ K:	I Am Kind	41
☐ **L**:	I Am Loved	45
☐ M:	I Am Mindful	49
☐ **N**:	I Am Needed	53

☐ O: I Am Observant   57

☐ P: I Am Patient   61

☐ Q: I Am Quirky   65

☐ R: I Am Responsible   69

☐ S: I Am Strong   73

☐ T: I Can Trust   77

☐ U: I Can Understand   81

☐ V: I Am Valuable   85

☐ W: I Can Wonder   89

☐ X: I Can Explore   93

☐ Y: I Am Yours   97

☐ Z: I Am Zealous   101

☐ Bonus Devotional: I Am Me!   105

Song Lyric Appendix   109

About the Author   116

NOTE TO FAMILIES

Jesus said, "Let the little children come to me, and do not hinder them, for the kingdom of heaven belongs to such as these."
MATTHEW 19:14 NIV

Dear Families and Caregivers,

Have you ever bought a new toy only to find your little ones liked the shipping box best? Or have you heard the uncontrollable giggles that come with switching a flashlight on and off fifty-plus times? Young children don't need that expensive, popular toy to learn. They just need freedom to discover and play. Often, the richest learning experiences come from exploring everyday items with loved ones—like a big brown box and a flashlight.

Educators know that young children learn academic and social concepts best through exploration and play. So it follows that our kids will also more fully understand faith concepts through hands-on fun. In Matthew 19, Jesus reminds us to let children come to Him without limitations. When we give young children static materials like worksheets to learn about God, we can unintentionally hinder them because they don't naturally learn by sitting still and completing tasks. Instead, children will flourish in their knowledge of God and in their faith when we allow them to use God's gift of curiosity and explore with their five senses.

I've seen this principle prove true in my own life as an educator and as a mom of a son who is autistic and has cerebral palsy. Through working with several wonderful therapists and learning to be an effective teacher, I noticed that the ways we try to teach children don't always match their needs. We are hindering them when we mean to help!

Being a parent is the most rewarding and challenging thing I have ever done. I'm sure many of you feel the same. We want so badly to give our kids the tools and training for success, but there are endless conflicting messages about what those tools are. Most of the time, it's simpler than all those guidebooks, social media photos, and "experts" would have us believe. My two boys, niece, and nephew taught me very quickly that hands-on learning also needs to be minds-on learning. Letting children discover, make choices, and share their ideas is what matters most. My goal didn't need to be that picture-perfect craft on social media. Sometimes the best result is a mess: a card that turns into a scribbled, heartfelt letter covering my carefully prepared construction paper cutout. Or the time we planned on making the perfect Wookie-Cookie only to discover sweeping up chocolate chips was the real fun.

I created this book to teach foundational biblical truths through simple, hands-on, minds-on explorations. I have also written it with a spirit of inclusion. Most of the activities will be successful with a variety of kids and types of family or group structures. But I acknowledge the blessing that God has made each of us and each of our family units unique. So if you see a way to adapt a project to better fit your child or your group size, go for it!

Once when my family was going through a difficult diagnosis process, a fellow parent of a special-needs child reminded me that our children are God's children first. He loves them all. Regardless of who makes up your family and each of your unique needs, I hope that with love, togetherness, and sensory play, we can make a path for the little children to come to Jesus.

With love,
Allison

HOW TO USE THIS BOOK

How do we encourage little children to explore BIG ideas? Develop a routine of exploring *together* using curiosity, exploration, and play! This book's structure will help you get in the rhythm of faith explorations. Each entry focuses on a letter of the alphabet and includes these elements:

- "God Made Me" affirmation
- short scripture
- bite-size devotional
- focus activity
- optional additional activities
- questions
- simple prayer

Some of the activities include singing a familiar children's song. If you don't already know the words, check the back of this book for a Song Lyric Appendix.

I've written these pieces to be flexible, so please mix and match to create a fun experience for your very special and

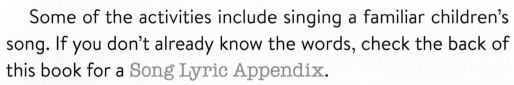

very unique little one. Here are three tips as you go along this fun faith journey together:

1. **Start anywhere.** You don't have to work through the alphabet from beginning to end. Encourage your child to help you choose the next "I Am" word. Keep track of your progress with the checklist Table of Contents in the beginning of the book.

2. **You don't need to do it all.** This book shares *a lot* of activities to give you a choice, not to keep you busy! Do the projects you love and save or skip the rest. You also don't need to do one letter in one day. Find the routine that works best for your family. Spread the fun over a few days or an entire week.

3. **Explore together.** This book provides opportunities for your child to unplug, slow down, and make meaningful memories. Join in as they explore faith, have fun, and connect with their loving Father God. The best thing we can give our children is ourselves. Be silly, laugh, talk, sing, play, and pray *together*.

As your family makes your way through the adventures in this book, you will create memories that will stick with your child for a lifetime. Treasure these little moments and have fun!

I AM
ADVENTUROUS

In the beginning God created
the sky and the earth.
Genesis 1:1

God wants to give you fun adventures. He wants you to learn about His world. He wants you to enjoy plants and animals and sunshine and rain. He wants you to make friends. You can go on an adventure right now! Go outside. Read a book. Try a new food. Ask an adult a question. God's good adventures are everywhere.

God makes beautiful things! What pretty things do you see outside that God made?

ADVENTURE HUNT

MATERIALS: basket or bag

Bring a basket or bag outside. Collect anything you like. Look for . . .

- your favorite color
- your favorite shape
- something you've never seen before

Describe It
- What color is it?
- What size is it?
- How does it feel?

Table Talk
Keep adding treasures to your basket. At mealtimes, show your family new items. Then thank God for your adventures.

Adventure Jar

Write easy adventures on paper slips, and put them in a jar. Each week, choose an adventure from the jar. Here are some ideas to get you started:

- Try a new food.
- Dance in the rain.
- Go to a park.
- Learn about an animal.
- Check out a book from the library.

Sing "The Itsy Bitsy Spider" with hand motions.

The itsy bitsy spider went on an adventure! When the rain washed her out, she tried again. When did you have to try again?

Dear God,
Thank You for adventures! I'm glad You are with me as I explore. Amen.

I AM BRAVE

"Be strong and brave. So don't be afraid. The Lord your God will be with you everywhere you go."
Joshua 1:9

God helps us be strong and brave. What does it mean to "be strong"? Sometimes being strong means lifting heavy things. Sometimes being strong means facing your fears. Are you afraid of high places, new people, or loud noises? You can do scary things because God is with you. When you feel afraid, tell an adult you love. Say a prayer together, and ask God to help you be brave.

When did you need bravery this week?

BALANCE BEAM

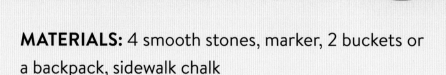

MATERIALS: 4 smooth stones, marker, 2 buckets or a backpack, sidewalk chalk

Think of 4 things that are hard for you. Ask an adult to write them on the stones. Or draw them. Place the stones into the buckets or pack. Chalk a long line on the ground. Carry the stones as you travel straight down the line. Ask for God's help to be strong and brave as you carry your heavy stones to the other side!

Bravery Badge

1. Cut out a big star from thick paper.
2. Add a heart to remind you that God is with you.
3. Add a string to wear your badge.

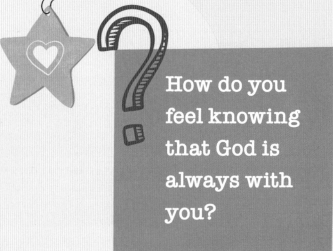

How do you feel knowing that God is always with you?

Brave Breathing

B Put your hand on your belly.

R Relax your shoulders.

A Breathe in all the way.

V Very slowly

E Exhale.

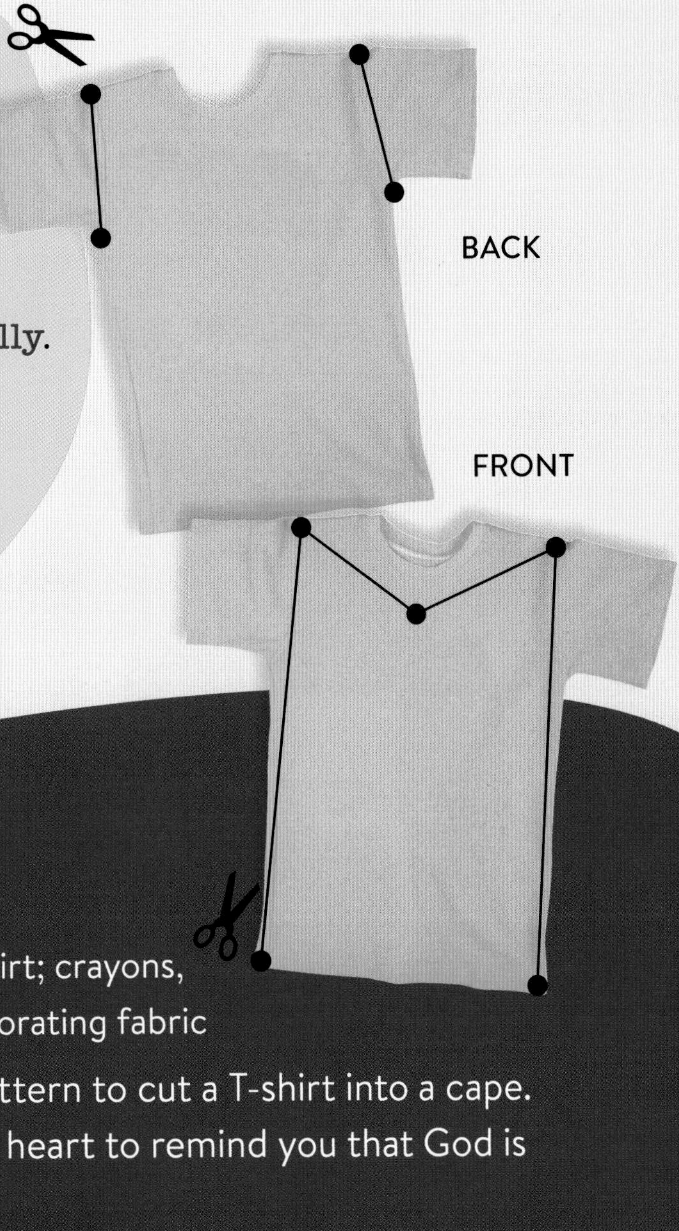

BACK

FRONT

Hero Cape

MATERIALS: oversized T-shirt; crayons, markers, or stickers for decorating fabric

Ask an adult to use the pattern to cut a T-shirt into a cape. Decorate the cape. Add a heart to remind you that God is always with you.

Dear God,
   I can be strong and brave with You. Amen.

I AM CREATIVE

All things were made through Him.
John 1:3

God gives everyone skills they are good at. Do you have a talent for making art? Are you good at making friends or making people laugh? Do you sing? We call these special talents *gifts* because they come from God. These skills are gifts because they make you happy. And your talents can be gifts to others when you use them to make people happy. God gives us gifts, and He wants us to use them to bless others.

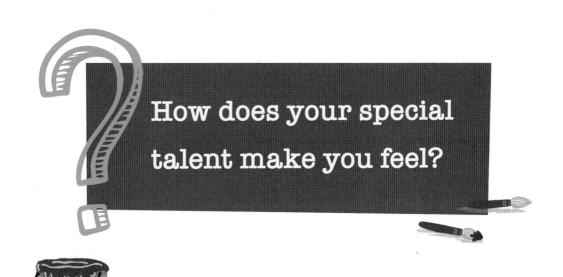

How does your special talent make you feel?

PUPPET STORY TIME

MATERIALS: small paper bag, crayons, craft supplies, scissors, glue

Create a puppet of your favorite animal. Ask an adult to read you the story of Noah and the ark while you work. Then use your puppet to tell the story yourself.

Build a Boat

Use aluminum foil to build a bowl-shaped boat. Test your boat in the sink. Does it float? Will it hold a small toy animal? If not, how can you make it stronger?

Noah was good at building. Who did he help by building the ark?

Sing "A Man Named Noah Built a Boat" to the tune of "Old MacDonald Had a Farm." Make up motions for each animal.

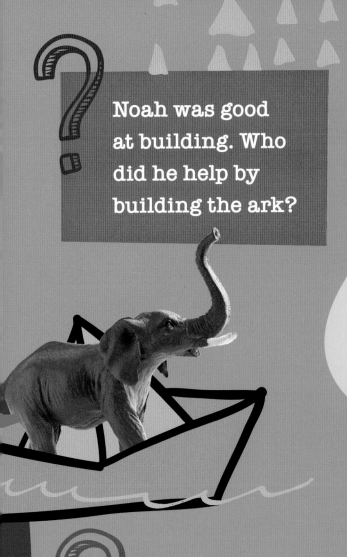

What other things come in twos?

(socks, shoes, gloves, earrings, etc.)

Dear God,
Thank You for my gifts! Show me ways to use my talents to bring joy. Amen.

I CAN DISCOVER

The Lord does great things. Those people who love them think about them.

Psalm 111:2

God gave us a world of great things to discover. *Discover* means to find or learn something new. You can discover anytime, anywhere. At bath time you may discover that some toys make a BIG splash and others make a tiny splash. Discovering is fun. It makes you smile. It can also bring you closer to God as you learn about the world He created.

What have you discovered this week?

DINO DISCOVERY BIN

MATERIALS:

box or container, 1 sheet thick paper, glue

filling: rice, sand, dried pasta, Easter grass, etc.

scraps: paper, buttons, craft sticks, yogurt caps, pipe cleaners, etc.

tools: spoon, brush, tongs, etc.

Dig up a dinosaur discovery! With your hands and tools, uncover the hidden objects. Then use your discoveries to build a dinosaur. Choose a piece for the head. Which parts make a good body, legs, and tail? Glue the parts onto the paper to create your own dinosaur sculpture.

How are your discoveries alike? How are they different?

Top Secret

Place 5 small toys in the discovery bin. Ask a friend to close their eyes and pull out a toy. As they keep their eyes closed, give 3 clues about what the toy is. Can they guess the toy? Take turns being the discoverer and clue giver.

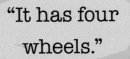

"It has four wheels."

"It is fast."

"Mommy drives one."

What discovery are you thankful for?

Hide-and-Seek

Have you ever discovered a lost toy in a hidden spot like under the couch? Discovering things we love makes us happy. Play hide-and-seek using your favorite toy with someone you love.

Dear God,
Thank You for creating an amazing world full of discoveries. Amen.

I AM EXCITED

Enjoy serving the Lord. And he
will give you what you want.
Psalm 37:4

Surprises are exciting. Have you ever woken up to your favorite yummy breakfast? Or maybe you found a lizard or a purple flower. It's also exciting to give other people happy surprises. God gives us exciting surprises every day.

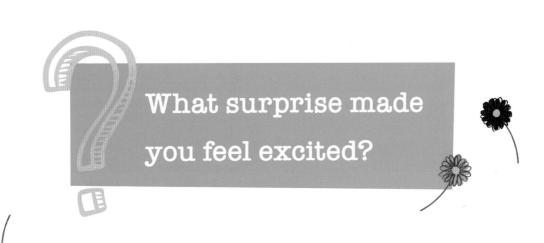

What surprise made
you feel excited?

MAGIC PEPPER

MATERIALS: 2 cups water, pie plate, ground pepper, cotton swab, dish soap

1. Pour water in a pie plate.
2. Shake pepper onto the water until the surface is mostly covered.
3. Dip an end of the swab in the dish soap.
4. Dip the swab in the water.
5. Surprise!

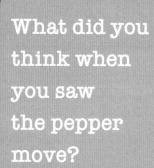

What did you think when you saw the pepper move?

Sing "If You're Happy and You Know It." Make up your own verses and motions.

Secret Surprise

- Do a chore when you weren't asked.
- Pick a flower for a friend or family member.
- Make a card for a neighbor.

Let's Do It!

Write or draw a list of 5 exciting activities. Pick 1 to do soon. Here are a few examples:

- Go to a playground.
- Have a dance party.
- Make pancakes.

How do you feel when you give someone a gift?

Dear God,
Thank You for surprises and excitement. Amen.

I Am Faithful

We live by what we believe,
not by what we can see.
2 Corinthians 5:7

Do you know the story of baby Moses? This Bible story reminds us to have faith in God. *Faith* means believing that God is with us.

The king had made a law that put babies in danger. So Moses' mother hid him in a basket. Then Moses' big sister, Miriam, set the basket in the river. Miriam hid in the grass and watched. She had faith that God would help. God led the king's daughter to the river. She found baby Moses and adopted him as her son. God saved baby Moses! You can have faith that God will help you too.

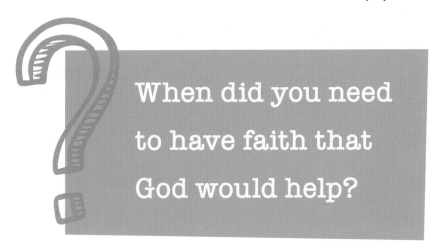

When did you need to have faith that God would help?

Story Basket

MATERIALS: basket, baby doll, small blanket, blue paper or towel, green paper strips

Wrap your baby in a blanket, and lay them in the basket. Spread your blue paper or towel like a river. Wave the paper strips like tall grass. Tell the story of baby Moses.

Hiding Heart

MATERIALS: white crayon, white paper, watercolors, paintbrush

Draw a white heart on the paper. Paint the paper and watch the heart appear. Just like the hiding heart, God is always here.

Cuddle and sing "Rock-a-Bye Baby" with your favorite person or toy. Then change the words to "Rock-a-Bye Moses" to tell the Bible story.

Rock-a-Bye Moses in the river.
As the water flows, the basket will rock.
God will watch over the baby inside
And keep him safe,
Warm, and dry.

Dear God,
Thank You for always being with me. Amen.

Paper Bag Basket

MATERIALS: large paper bag, 2 pipe cleaners, scissors, green paper strips, crayons (optional)

1. Cut the top ²/₃ off a paper bag. Color your basket if you'd like.
2. Cut holes in the 4 corners of the paper bag's long sides, about 1 inch below the top.
3. Thread the pipe cleaner ends through the holes to make a two handles.
4. Twist the pipe cleaner ends to secure.
5. Decorate with green paper grass.

I AM GRATEFUL

Let everything that breathes
praise the Lord.
Psalm 150:6

God takes care of us. He gives us things like food and your favorite stuffed animal. He also gives us time. Time to be with friends and family. Time to play. Time to sing. Time to hug your favorite adult. Time to splash in a pond. Be grateful and say "thank You" to God for all these blessings.

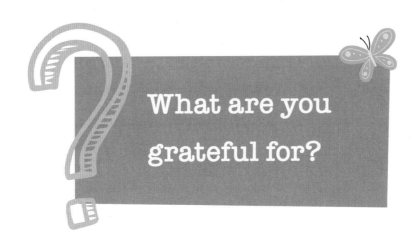

What are you grateful for?

GRATITUDE COLLAGE

MATERIALS: magazines or photographs, scissors, paper, glue

Gather magazines or photographs. Tear or cut out photos of things you are grateful for. Glue them on a piece of paper. Hang it up, and tell God "thank You" for one of the items each time you see it.

Praying Hand

MATERIALS: pencil, paper, crayons

Trace your hand or foot. Draw a happy face on it. Then thank God for what your body can do.

How do you feel when you think about your blessings?

Red, Yellow, and Blue Thank You

MATERIALS: bag or basket; red, blue, and yellow paper strips

Place colored paper strips in the bag. Take turns pulling out a color and sharing what you are grateful for.

Color Key
red: food or drink
blue: person or animal
yellow: special memory

Thankful Tree

MATERIALS: green paper, scissors, pencil, large stick or branch, string, vase

1. Cut leaves out of paper.
2. Write or draw things you are thankful for on the leaves.
3. Cut a hole in the top of each leaf, and tie it to the branch.
4. Put the branch in a vase on your dinner table.
5. At mealtimes, share the things you are grateful for.

Dear God,
  I am grateful for all the ways You show Your love to me. Amen.

I AM HOPEFUL

"I have good plans for you . . . to give
you hope and a good future."
Jeremiah 29:11

God loves when you smile and laugh. He wants you to play and be happy. He has good things planned for you! But you will still have bad days and sad times. And it's okay to feel frustrated or to cry sometimes. But remember that God has good plans. Just like a rainbow comes on a rainy day, God will bring good things again. Have hope in Him!

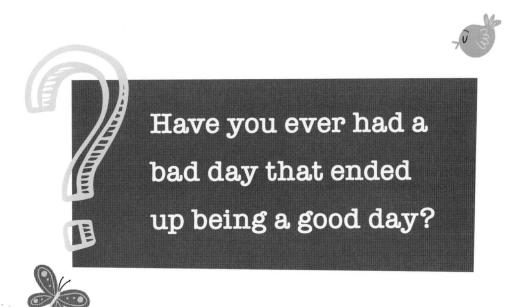

Have you ever had a
bad day that ended
up being a good day?

Rain Cloud Surprise

MATERIALS: black washable marker, coffee filter, spray bottle with water, towel

1. Draw a black cloud on the filter.
2. Spray the cloud with water 3–5 times.

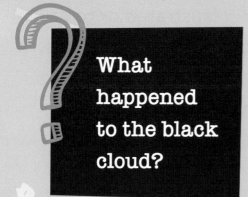

What happened to the black cloud?

Fruit Rainbow

MATERIALS: fruit in rainbow colors: red, orange, yellow, green, blue, purple; clear cup; whipped cream or vanilla yogurt

Layer the fruit in the cup in rainbow order. Top with whipped cream or yogurt. Enjoy!

Rainy Day Duck

MATERIALS: white paper plate; yellow, white, black, and orange paper; glue; scissors

Tear the yellow paper into small pieces. Glue it on the whole paper plate. Cut out 2 white circles. Cut out 2 smaller black circles. Glue the black circles on the white circles, then glue to the paper plate to make eyes. Cut out a duck bill from orange paper. Glue the bill below the eyes, hanging off the plate.

Sing "Rain, Rain, Go Away" while you pretend to splash in big puddles!

Rainbows remind us to hope in God's promises. What do you hope for this week?

Dear God,
Help me have hope on happy days and hard days. Amen.

I AM INCLUSIVE

Do not be interested only in your own life,
but be interested in the lives of others.
Philippians 2:4

God loves everyone. He loves the people in your family. He loves your friends. And He loves the people you don't know. God wants us to show kindness to everyone. We are all His children!

When you see a new person, there is an easy way to help them feel welcome and included. Smile and say hello!

Think of a friend. How are they like you? How are they different?

Have you ever been to a new place? How did you feel?

BREAD AND BUTTER

Once, the prophet Elijah asked a poor woman for bread. She was almost out of flour and oil. But she trusted God and made bread to share. Then God filled her jars with flour and oil!

MATERIALS: jar, heavy cream, bread

1. Fill your jar half full of cream.
2. Put the lid on tight.
3. Shake, shake, shake! Take turns and shake for 10–15 minutes.
4. Spread the butter on bread.
5. Share with a friend.

Friendship Bracelet

String beads on a piece of elastic thread, and tie the ends together. Give the bracelet to a new friend.

Even though we are different, we each have something special inside. What makes you special?

Apple Stars

MATERIALS: red apple, green apple, knife, cutting board

Slice the red apple horizontally, across the middle. What do you see inside? Now slice the green apple. Are they the same or different?

Hello!

Practice saying hello in different languages.

American Sign Language:

Spanish: Hola
German: Hallo
Swahili: Jambo
Chinese: Ni hao

Dear God,
 Thank You for always welcoming me and helping me welcome others. Amen.

I AM JOYFUL

Joy is a short word with a BIG meaning. Joy feels like happiness, but it stays in your heart when you have trouble.

Have you ever gotten a hug on a hard day? The hug didn't solve your problem, but it made you feel better, didn't it? That's also how God's love can make us feel. God loves you on good days and bad days. That's why you can always have joy.

When did you feel happy today?

FILLED WITH JOY

MATERIALS: empty plastic bottle, white vinegar, balloon, baking soda, funnel, spoon

PART 1

1. Fill the bottle ¼ full of vinegar.
2. Give your balloon a few stretches.
3. Insert a funnel into the balloon's opening. Pour 2 spoonfuls of baking soda into the balloon.
4. Keep the balloon tilted to the side so the baking soda stays in. Stretch the neck of the balloon around the bottle's mouth.
5. Lift the balloon up so the powder drops into the bottle.
6. Watch the balloon fill up!

PART 2

1. Stand really tall.
2. Say, "I am God's child."
3. Now imagine your lungs are balloons, and take a giant breath.

Do you feel stronger and ready for your next adventure? You're filled with joy!

Sing "I've Got the Joy." Now sing the lyrics in silly voices: as a robot, a scuba diver, a mouse.

Sprouting Joy

Joy can grow in your heart—just like a plant grows from a tiny seed!

MATERIALS: 3—5 dried lima beans, water, paper towel, plastic zip bag

1. Soak beans in water overnight.
2. Dampen your paper towel. Place it in the bag.
3. Place the beans on the paper towel.
4. Seal the bag.
5. Place the bag in a warm, sunny spot.
6. Watch your seeds sprout!

How do you feel when you make a friend smile?

Building Blocks Game

Take turns with a friend stacking blocks to build a tower. Each time you add a block, share something about God, like "God loves me" or "God is with me."

Dear God,
Thank You that I can have joy every day
because You love me. Amen.

I AM KIND

"Love each other as I have loved you."
John 13:34

One day Jesus was teaching when the listening crowd got hungry. Jesus found one basket of bread and fish. He handed out the food in pieces. The food fed everyone! Jesus did a miracle to take care of the people. Jesus was always kind.

God wants you to be kind like Jesus. Share your crayons. Help someone who falls. Say "thank you." You can help others and show love, just like Jesus.

What are two kind things you can do this week?

MUFFINS WITH LOVE

You can't feed a crowd with one basket of food like Jesus, but you can make food to share. Get an adult to help you bake muffins and bring them to a friend, neighbor, or relative.

INGREDIENTS

2 cups flour

3 teaspoons baking powder

$1/2$ teaspoon salt

$2/3$ cup sugar

1 egg

1 cup milk

$1/4$ cup melted butter

optional mix-ins: 1 cup chocolate chips, fruit, or nuts

DIRECTIONS

1. Preheat oven to 400 degrees.
2. In a large bowl, mix flour, baking powder, salt, and sugar.
3. In another bowl, beat egg with milk and butter.
4. Pour the egg mixture into the flour. Stir to make a thick, lumpy batter.
5. Stir in any mix-ins.
6. Spoon batter into the cups of a muffin tin until they are $3/4$ full.
7. Bake 25 minutes.

Kindness Chain Challenge

Each time you catch someone in your family being kind, write or draw the action on a strip of paper. Loop the strips to make a kindness chain. Make the chain bigger and bigger!

Sprinkle Kindness

Fill a plastic zip bag with sprinkles and seal. Use your finger to draw the shapes listed below in the sprinkles. As you draw, think of kind actions you can do.

house: at home
cross: in your neighborhood
heart: for family members
circle: for friends

Mirror Messages

Look in a mirror and practice saying kind words to yourself.

- "God loves me just as I am."
- "We all make mistakes. I'm learning."
- "I am kind."

Dear God,
   I'm so glad You are kind. Help me be kind to others and to myself. Amen.

L

I AM LOVED

We love because God first loved us.
1 John 4:19

God's love for us is BIG. It's bigger than the ocean. Bigger than outer space. Bigger than *anything*. God made us to love others just like He loves us. We love our family. We love our friends. We love our pets or favorite toys. We love our homes and the earth. And because God's big love never ends, our love for others will never be all used up.

Who do you love?

How Big Is Your Hug?

MATERIALS: wrapping paper, marker, measuring tape

1. Unroll a long strip of paper on the ground.
2. Lie down with your head below the top of the paper, and stretch out your arms.
3. Ask a friend to trace around your head and arms.
4. Measure your hug from hand to hand.
5. Take turns tracing and measuring each person's hug.

Heart Art

MATERIALS: paper, scissors, tape, paint, paintbrush

Cut out a heart. Lightly tape the back of the heart onto a sheet of paper. Paint the paper all around the heart. Let the paint dry. Pull the heart off to see your heart art.

Who has the longest hug? Who has the shortest hug?

Red Reminder

Paint a heart on a small stone. When the paint is dry, put the stone in your pocket or backpack. Whenever you see it, remember that God loves you. Make another heart stone for a friend, or leave one as a surprise in a park or on a sidewalk.

How do you show your love to others?

Sing "Jesus Loves the Little Children."

Dear God,
Thank You for loving me **BIG**!
Show me ways to love others. Amen.

I AM MINDFUL

1 Peter 5:7

God sees your smiles. He sees your frowns and tears. He sees your mad faces and your stomping feet.

God made us to have different feelings. But sometimes our feelings get **BIG**. Then we need help to calm down. You can give your big feelings to God. He will listen to you and calm your feelings with His **GIANT** peace.

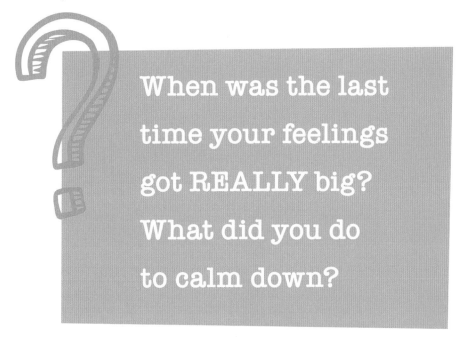

When was the last time your feelings got REALLY big? What did you do to calm down?

BUBBLE BREATHING

MATERIALS:

bubble solution: ¾ cup water mixed with 1 tablespoon dish soap

bubble wand: a pipe cleaner formed into a circle with a handle

1. Dip your wand in the bubble solution.
2. Close your eyes, and tell God how you feel.
3. Take a big breath, and blow into the wand SLOOOOWLY.
4. Open your eyes, and watch your bubbles fly.
5. Thank God for taking your big feelings.

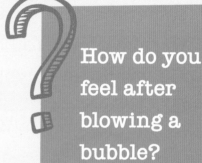

How do you feel after blowing a bubble?

Heart Breath

MATERIALS: pipe cleaner, paper, glue

1. Form a heart shape with a pipe cleaner.
2. Glue the heart on a piece of paper.
3. Trace one side of the heart with your finger as you breathe in deeply. Trace the other side, and breathe out slowly.

3, 2, 1 Sensory Walk

Take a walk outside with someone. Share 3 things you see, 2 things you hear, and 1 thing you smell.

Calm Bottle

MATERIALS: empty plastic water bottle; water; glitter, mini pom-poms, or small plastic toys; food coloring; baby oil; glue

1. Fill a clean water bottle ⅔ full of water.
2. Add glitter, mini pom-poms, or small plastic toys.
3. Add a few drops of food coloring.
4. Fill the bottle to the top with baby oil.
5. Glue on the lid, and shake!

Dear God,
Sometimes my feelings are BIG. Thank You for helping me calm down. Amen.

I AM NEEDED

Let us think about each other and help each other to show love and do good deeds.
Hebrews 10:24

Coaches are team leaders who teach you to play a sport. They help you work together with your teammates. But even if you don't play a sport, you are on a team—God's team.

God has formed a team of friends and family for you. Maybe they count on you to help sort the laundry or tell silly jokes or give an encouraging hug. You are needed on your team!

What do you do to help your team of family and friends?

PARACHUTE PLAYTIME

MATERIALS: bedsheet, stuffed animal, 4 or more people

1. Spread out the bedsheet.
2. Place the stuffed animal in the center.
3. Have each person hold on to the sheet's edge until all 4 sides are off the ground.
4. Bounce the stuffed animal . . .

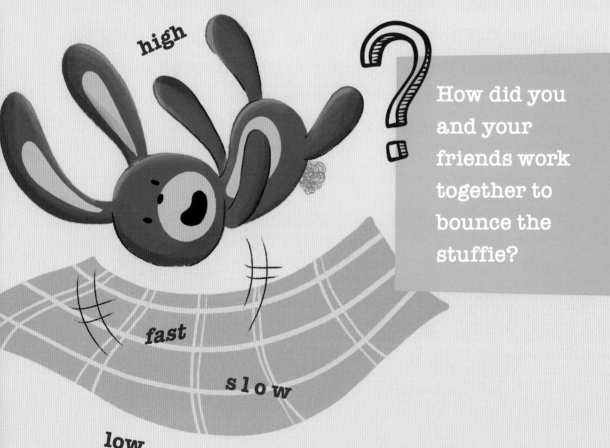

high

fast

slow

low

How did you and your friends work together to bounce the stuffie?

Bowling

MATERIALS: 6 empty water bottles or paper cups, small ball

1. Set up the water bottles or cups in a bowling triangle.
2. Roll the ball toward the "pins."
3. For each "pin" you knock down, share a way you can help a friend, family member, or neighbor.

Secret Helper

Glue 2 craft sticks together to make a cross. Then look for sneaky ways to be kind. Leave the cross out when you secretly sweep the floor, pick up your brother's mess, or leave a wildflower on your mom's desk.

Super Star

Make a trophy or medal for a friend or family member. Name the award, and surprise them with it.

Hug Hero   Funniest Jokes
Star Cook   Tallest Towers

Dear God,

You are a good leader. Thank You for coaching me as I learn to help others on my team. Amen.

I AM OBSERVANT

The Lord has made both these things: Ears that can hear and eyes that can see.
Proverbs 20:12

God made you exactly as you are. He made you curious. And He gave you five senses to use to make discoveries. Eyes see colorful rainbows. Noses smell flowers. Tongues pucker at sour lemons. Toes feel bumpy rocks. Ears hear squirrels chattering. God gave us so many ways to explore the world He made.

Would you rather feel warm sunshine or a cool breeze?

Little Light of Mine Lightning Bug

MATERIALS: empty water bottle, construction paper, tape, 4 pipe cleaners cut in half, black marker, glow stick

God made light. Light helps our eyes see what is around us. And light helps us communicate. Did you know that fireflies shine tiny lights to find each other?

1. Cut 4 long paper ovals to make wings. Tape 2 wings on each side of the bottle.
2. Bend pipe cleaners to shape antennae and legs. Tape them to the bottle.
3. Draw 2 eyes with the marker.
4. Bend your glow stick to make it glow, and place it inside the bottle.
5. Put on the bottle cap.

Smell or taste: Which sense is your favorite to use in the kitchen?

What's That Taste?

Ask a friend or grown-up to put different foods on a plate. Close your eyes as you taste each food. Is it sweet, salty, sour, or bitter? Guess what each food is.

Which food did you like the best?

Sing "This Little Light of Mine."

Scratch-and-Sniff Art

MATERIALS: paper, glue, flavored gelatin powder

1. Draw a picture or write your name with glue.
2. Cover the glue with gelatin powder.
3. After it dries, scratch and smell your art!

Dear God,
   I love observing the world You made by seeing, hearing, smelling, touching, and tasting. Thank You for giving me so many ways to explore. Amen.

I AM PATIENT

But we are hoping for something that we do not have yet. We are waiting for it patiently.
Romans 8:25

Sometimes we want things to happen right *now*. You might want to build a castle, but your friend is playing with the blocks. So to be kind, you wait. Or you want it to be your birthday *today*! You have to wait because it's not the right time. Or you want to swim, but it's storming. You wait to be safe.

It is hard to wait. Waiting can even make you feel stormy, with frustration and excitement blowing around inside you. But God wants us to stay calm and kind as we wait. That's called *patience*!

When was a time you felt stormy inside because you had to wait?

RAINSTORM IN A JAR

MATERIALS: jar, water, food coloring, shaving cream, small cup, medicine dropper

1. Fill the jar nearly to the top with water.
2. Add a shaving cream cloud to the top.
3. Mix together ½ cup of water and 10 drops of food coloring in a small cup.
4. Drop colored water onto the cloud.

Wait and watch as you keep dropping colored water.

A Tall-as-Me Tower

Use paper cups to build a tower that's as tall as you! Work with a friend. Take turns adding one cup at a time until your tower is all done.

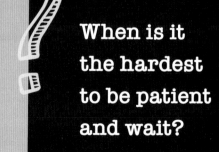

When is it the hardest to be patient and wait?

I Spy

The next time you have to wait, choose something to look for.

- clouds shaped like animals
- items of a certain color
- things that start with a letter of the alphabet
- things that could be worn as a hat

Dear God,
   Help me find fun things to do when I have to wait. Amen.

Rainy Day Jar

On strips of paper, write indoor activities that make you happy or calm. Put the ideas inside a jar. The next time it rains or you feel stormy inside, pull out a paper and do the activity. For example . . .

- Read a book.
- Listen to music.
- Bake muffins.
- Build a block city.

I AM QUIRKY

I praise you because you made me in
an amazing and wonderful way.
Psalm 139:14

God made you quirky. That means you aren't like anyone else. And that's wonderful!

Maybe you know hundreds of animal facts. Maybe you like to draw pictures for your friends. Maybe you love to wear your favorite fuzzy socks or bright red shoes. God made you in a wonderfully special way, and He loves all your quirks exactly as He made them.

God made animals quirky too! Dragonflies can fly backward. Zebras have zany stripes. God's creations are all are amazing.

What about yourself makes you feel special?

GORILLA NOSEPRINT MASK

Did you know a gorilla's noseprint is as unique as a human's fingerprint? No two are alike.

MATERIALS: paper plate, black paint, gray paper, marker

1. Paint the plate black, and set aside.
2. From the paper, cut a heart with a rounded bottom.
3. Dip a finger in the paint. Press it in the middle of the paper twice in a V-shape to make a nose.
4. Draw a mouth.
5. Cut out 2 white circles. Add dots for eyes.
6. Glue the eyes to the face. Glue the face onto the plate.

What does your fingerprint look like? Are the lines curvy or straight?

Chameleon Tongue

Cut a piece of string as long as your body. That is how long your tongue would be if you were a chameleon!

Ants on a Log

Giant anteaters eat up thousands of insects a day! Spread nut or seed butter on top of a piece of celery. Line up raisins on the butter. Enjoy, little anteater!

Cheetah, Sloth

Glue a cheetah picture on a paper plate. Glue a sloth picture on the back. When you see the cheetah, run fast. When you see the sloth, creep slowly.

Dear God,
Thank You for making me special. Help me love myself as You made me. Amen.

What are three ways God made you quirky?

I AM RESPONSIBLE

In all the work you are doing,
work the best you can.
Colossians 3:20

God made you to be a helper. You can put your dirty clothes in the laundry basket. You can feed a pet. You can help clean up when you spill. Being responsible means helping and cleaning up after yourself. There are many ways to be responsible every day.

How will you be a helper this week?

SORTING SOCKS

MATERIALS: 2 baskets or bins, clean socks

You can help with the laundry! You can sort. You can fold. You can put clean clothes away.

1. Put the little socks in one basket. Put the big socks in the other basket.
2. For each basket, find exact matches and fold them together.
3. Make a pile of your socks. Put them away.

Car Wash

Play with toy cars in the dirt. Then wash them in a pan of soapy water with an old toothbrush or cloth.

How does it feel when you help do chores?

Sweep, Sweep

MATERIALS: cereal, small broom, dustpan, container

Spread the cereal on the floor. Sweep it up! Pour the cereal into a container to reuse when you want to sweep again.

Sing these lyrics to the tune of "Row, Row, Row, Your Boat."

Scrub, scrub, scrub your hands.
Get 'em really clean.
Dry, dry, dry, 'em off.
I can take care of me.

How do you help pick up after yourself?

Dear God,
Help me learn to take care of myself and my world. Amen.

I AM STRONG

I can do all things through Christ
because he gives me strength.
Philippians 4:13

Do you know someone who can pick you up and toss you in the air? That person is strong! You can be strong too. God makes your mind strong. You can think through problems and solve them. You can learn to put on your socks and shoes all by yourself. God makes your heart strong. You can say goodbye to a friend even though it makes you feel sad. You can do hard things because you are strong.

Even when you can't do a hard thing, God can. He is stronger than anyone else, and He is always here to help you.

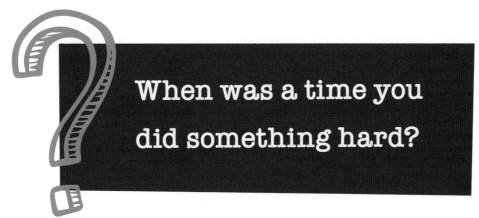

When was a time you did something hard?

STONES OF HELP

MATERIALS: rocks of varying sizes

In the Bible, a people made piles of stones called *stones of help* to remember times the Lord helped them. You can build your own pile to remember the Lord's help.

1. Find a place to build your stones of help.
2. Stack your stones from largest to smallest.
3. Each time you place a stone, share one way God has helped you.
4. When you pass by, tell God thank You for being strong and helping you.

How has God helped you?

Sing "I'm in the Lord's Army" as you march, ride, and zoom.

Prayer Path

Draw a giant spiral outside with sidewalk chalk. Start on the outside and talk to God as you walk toward the center. Thank Him for helping you be strong, or ask Him to help you with a problem.

Catapult

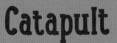

MATERIALS: serving spoon, toilet paper roll, 2 rubber bands, cotton balls

Crisscross the rubber bands to secure the middle of the spoon to the paper roll. Place a cotton ball in the spoon. Hit the end of the spoon and see how far you can launch the cotton ball.

Dear God,
    Thank You for helping me be strong: strong in my body and strong in my heart. Amen.

I CAN
TRUST

Trust the Lord with all your heart.
Proverbs 3:5

The Bible story of Jonah shows us that God is trustworthy. God asked Jonah to go to a dangerous city. Jonah thought God's direction was a bad idea! So he got on a boat traveling far away. But a storm came, and Jonah was swallowed by a whale. Inside the whale, Jonah prayed. He told God he was sorry for not trusting. God listened. God told the whale to spit Jonah out on a beach. After that, Jonah obeyed God and went to the city.

Did someone tell you to do something today that you did NOT want to do? Did you shout "no!" or cry? Your family still loves you. God still loves you. Say sorry. Then ask God to help you do the right thing. He will take care of you as you do it.

What do your parents or teachers ask you to do that you don't like? Why don't you like that task? Why do they ask you to do it?

WHALE BELLY TENT

MATERIALS: large blanket, 4 chairs, Bible or Bible storybook, paper, crayons

1. Place four chairs in a large square.
2. Spread the blanket over the chairs to make a tent.
3. Read the story of Jonah.
4. Draw a whale as you pray. Tell God about the things you don't like to do. Ask Him to help you trust Him and the grown-ups who take care of you.

Moon Sand

Mix 4 cups of flour and ½ cup of oil to make your own sand.

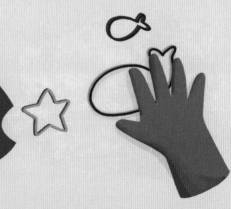

Whale Blanket

Whales have blubber, a thick layer of fat. God gave whales blubber to keep them warm in the cold ocean. Blubber is like a whale's blanket.

MATERIALS: bowl of ice water, plastic baggie, shortening, plastic glove

1. Fill a plastic baggie with shortening.
2. Put on the glove, and then put your hand in the blubber bag.
3. Plunge your "blubber" hand into the ice water, and count to 10.
4. Take your hand out of the ice water and out of the glove.
5. Put your bare hand in the ice water, and count to 10.

How did your hand feel with and without the blubber blanket?

Go Fish

Play Go Fish with a deck of cards.

Dear God,
Help me obey and trust that You are always taking care of me. Amen.

I Can Understand

Be happy with those who are happy.
Be sad with those who are sad.
Romans 12:15

God understands how you feel. Your smile makes Him happy. When you are sad, He is sad too.

God wants you to understand how others feel. When your friend is happy, does it make you smile? It's good to celebrate good things with friends. When your friend is crying, do you feel sad? It's good to cry with a friend or give them a hug. When we understand and love each other, we show God's love.

When have you celebrated with a friend?

Egg-sploring Empathy

MATERIALS: 2 plastic eggs, cotton ball, small rock, marker

1. When you are silly with your friends, you feel happy! You feel light! You might even feel cuddly, like a cotton ball. Put the cotton ball in an egg. Draw a happy face on the egg.
2. When you are with someone who is sad, you feel heavy. You might feel cold or hard, like a rock. Put the rock in the second egg. Draw a sad face on it.
3. Take turns with each egg. When you hold the happy egg, think of one thing to say to or do for a friend who is happy. When you hold the sad egg, think of one thing to say to or do for a friend who is sad.

Good Listener

MATERIALS: 3 plastic eggs, cereal, rice, cotton balls

Fill three plastic eggs: one with cereal, one with rice, and one with cotton balls. Give each one a shake. Which egg sounds the loudest? Which sounds the softest?

Egg-cellent Friend

Think of a friend who might need a smile. Make them a card.

Help Humpty Dumpty

MATERIALS: white paper, scissors, pencil, tape

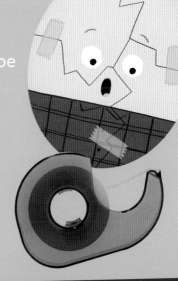

1. Cut an oval out of white paper.
2. Draw a face on the egg shape.
3. Tear it into five pieces.
4. Put the pieces back in the right places, and tape together.

What do you want someone to do when you are happy? What about when you are sad?

Dear God,
   Thank You for understanding how I feel. Help me be a good friend and treat others with understanding. Amen.

I AM VALUABLE

I have written your name on my hand.
Isaiah 49:16

God created you, and He knows your name. He knows everything about you. He knows you love swimming or dancing or drawing or fishing. He knows your favorite book. He knows the foods you love. He knows the foods you don't love. He loves you when you are kind and helpful. He loves you when you are grouchy. It doesn't matter what you do. You matter to God. He made you. You are very valuable to Him.

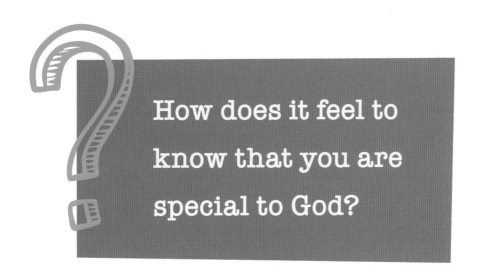

How does it feel to know that you are special to God?

BAG BUDDY

The Bible says that God knows how many hairs you have on your head. Wow!

MATERIALS: paper bag, marker, scissors

1. Draw a face on your bag.
2. Use scissors to cut downward from the top of the bag to create strips of hair.
3. Count how many hairs are on your Bag Buddy's head.

What else do you think God knows about you?

Pizza Time

God gives everyone a special purpose. Make a pizza together. Give each person their own job, such as spreading the sauce, sprinkling the cheese, and adding the meat. Eat and enjoy!

I Am Handy

Trace your hand on a piece of paper. Write your name on the hand. Decorate the page with pictures that show ways you are special.

How does it feel to make something together?

Sing "His Banner Over Me Is Love."

Dear God,
I matter to You. Thank You for loving me all the time. Amen.

I Can Wonder

Only the Lord gives wisdom. Knowledge and understanding come from Him.
Proverbs 2:6

God made you curious. And He loves to share His world with you. God wants you to wonder, ask questions, and learn. Why does it rain? What sound does a hippo make? Why does it snow only when it's cold out? Why are rocks all different colors? Wondering is a gift from God. When you learn about God's world, you learn more about Him!

What have you wondered today?

SUMMER SNOW

When it's cold out, rain freezes and turns into snowflakes.

   With this snow recipe, you can play with snow even when it's warm out!

MATERIALS: large bin, 1 cup shaving cream, 1 cup baking soda

1. Mix shaving cream and baking soda in a large bin.
2. Play with your snow. Scoop, pour, and build like you would in a sandbox. Or create a wintry scene with small toys.

Sing "The Wise Man Built His House Upon the Rock."

Why is it wise to build a house on rock? How is God like a rock?

Root Beer Float

God made the world with three kinds of materials: solids, liquids, and gases. A root beer float is a special treat that has all three! Ice cream is a solid. Root beer is a liquid. And when you put them together, they make gas bubbles. *Fizzzzz!*

Rock Wonders

Look at sand and rocks in a magnifying glass. What do you notice? What do you wonder about them?

Dear God,
I am curious. Thank You for giving me the ability to wonder and learn. Amen.

I CAN EXPLORE

"For men this is impossible. But for God all things are possible."
Matthew 19:26

The Bible tells us how God created the world. He made night and day. He made the sun and the moon. He made water and land. He made every kind of plant and animal.

Then, last of all, God made people. He gave people five senses to experience His wonderful world. He gave people noses to smell flowers, fingers to feel wet sand, tongues to taste chocolate, eyes to see colorful flowers, and ears to hear owls hooting. God made us to be explorers!

Which sense is your favorite to use to explore a yummy treat?

STAR PROJECTOR

God made millions and billions of shining stars. You can make a star projector and create a twinkly night sky in your house.

MATERIALS: dark paper, pencil, flashlight, scissors, tape

1. On the paper, trace around the lens of the flashlight.
2. Cut out the circle.
3. Punch about 10 holes in the circle with your pencil.
4. Tape the circle over the lens of the flashlight.
5. Turn the flashlight on and shine your stars on the ceiling.

What's your favorite thing about the night? What's your favorite thing about the day?

Sing "Twinkle, Twinkle, Little Star."

Sailor's Suitcase

Play a silly sailor word game. Say, "I'm sailing a boat, and I'm going to take a _____." Take turns filling in the blank with a word that starts with the letters of the alphabet.

Would you rather explore space or the ocean?

Flower Garden

Use pipe cleaners to make flowers of many colors. Plant your flowers in jars or pots by burying the stems in rice, beans, or clay.

Dear God,
   Thank You for creating a wonderful world for me to explore. Amen.

I AM
YOURS

May the Lord bless and keep you.
Numbers 6:24

God made you. You are His child, and He is your Father. Close your eyes. Imagine bright sunlight on your face. He is the light. Imagine cuddling in a warm blanket. He is the softness and the warmth. Imagine two super strong arms wrapping you in a tight hug. He is the hug.

Do you feel a warm, happy feeling in your heart? It is wonderful to know that you belong to God. He is your Father in heaven, and He takes care of you. He keeps you safe. He brings you blessings. He makes wonderful plans of amazing things for you to do. He is always with you.

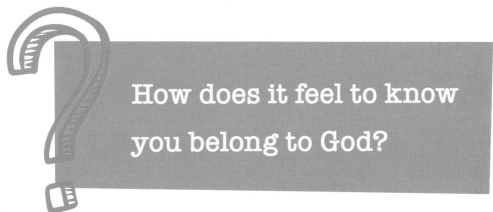

How does it feel to know you belong to God?

WRAPPED UP IN GOD'S LOVE

The cross is a symbol that helps us remember God's love.

MATERIALS: 2 sticks, large rubber band, yarn

1. Collect two sticks from outside.
2. Use the sticks to form a cross.
3. Wrap a rubber band around where the sticks cross.
4. Wrap the cross in yarn.
5. Hang your cross somewhere special.

Mirror Me

Use dry erase markers to draw yourself on a mirror. Take a photo of your artwork. (Be sure to turn off the flash!) Wipe off your portrait when you are finished.

Praying Hand

You can use your hand to help you pray.

- Thumb: Dear God,
- Pointer Finger: Thank You for _____.
- Middle Finger: Please help me/others _____.
- Ring Finger: Forgive me for _____.
- Pinky: In Jesus' name, amen.

Who would you like to pray for? How do you want someone to pray for you?

Sing "He's Got the Whole World in His Hands."

Dear God,
   I am Your child. Thank You for loving me and keeping me close. Amen.

I AM ZEALOUS

Sing and make music in your
hearts to the Lord.
Ephesians 5:19

Remember a time a friend said something nice about you. Maybe they said you were great at building with blocks. How does it feel when someone says something kind? It makes you smile! It makes your heart feel warm and happy. When you say or do nice things for God, it's called *praise*. There are different ways to give God praise. You can remember a time God helped you. You can draw a picture of a Bible story or a cool animal God made. One really fun way to praise God is to make music!

What is your favorite
song to sing really loud?

FEEL & SEE SOUND

Sound is made by movement. That means sometimes you can see and feel how sounds are made.

Hum: Place your fingertips on your throat and hum. What do you feel? That buzzing feeling is called *vibration*. When your throat vibrates, sound comes from your mouth.

Rubber Band Guitar: Stretch a rubber band over an open box. Pluck the rubber band. What does the rubber band do?

Drum: Flip over a plastic container. Find two big spoons. Drum the spoons on top. Can you see the container top move?

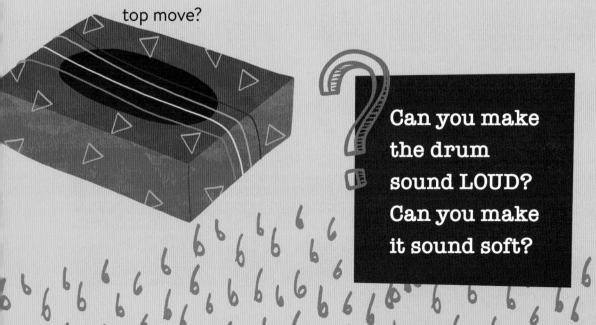

Can you make the drum sound LOUD? Can you make it sound soft?

Joyful Jingle

MATERIALS: 1 stick, pipe cleaner, jingle bells

1. Collect one stick.
2. Thread the jingle bells on the pipe cleaner.
3. Wrap your pipe cleaner around the stick.

Sing "The B-I-B-L-E" with your guitar, jingle stick, drum, or scarves.

Scarf Dance

Listen to your favorite song. As you listen, do these motions with scarves or small towels.

- Shake them high. Shake them low.
- Flap them like wings!
- Twirl them in circles.
- Wiggle them quickly. Wave them slowly.

Dear God,
    I love making music with You. Amen.

I AM ME!

Jesus said, "Let the little
children come to me."
Matthew 19:14

God made you with love. He made you kind. He made you curious. He made you a helper. He chose your eye color and hair color. He made you to be loud or quiet. He made you to love dinosaurs or building or dancing.

You are special to Jesus, and He wants to be near you. He wants you to talk to Him. He smiles when you smile. He wants to hug you when you feel sad. He loves you *all* the time. God made you to be exactly who you are.

What do you like best about you?

Name Bracelet

MATERIALS: elastic thread, scissors, letter beads for your name, colored beads

1. Cut a piece of thread 1 foot long.
2. String letter beads to spell your name.
3. Add beads of your favorite colors.
4. Tie knots on each side of the beads.
5. Tie the bracelet around your wrist.
6. Cut off any extra thread.

Compare your name to your friends' or family members' names. Whose name has the most letters?

"I Am" Poem

Write your name in a column with each letter on its own line. For each letter, write a word beginning with that letter that describes you.

Alphabet Soup

Put magnetic letters and pom-poms in a large bowl. Use a spoon to scoop out the letters of your name.

Sing "Jesus Loves Me" in American Sign Language.

Dear God,
Thank You for all the special ways You made me. I love You. Amen.

Song Lyric Appendix

The Itsy Bitsy Spider

The itsy bitsy spider climbed up the water spout.
Down came the rain and washed the spider out.
Out came the sun and dried up all the rain,
And the itsy bitsy spider went up the spout again.

A Man Named Noah Built a Boat

A man named Noah built a boat 'cause God told him so.
And on that boat, there were two CATS, E-I-E-I-O.
With a meow, meow here and a meow, meow there.
Here a meow, there a meow, everywhere a meow, meow.
A man named Noah built a boat 'cause God told him so.

Continue the song with other animals.

If You're Happy and You Know It

If you're happy and you know it, clap your hands.
If you're happy and you know it, clap your hands.
If you're happy and you know it and
you really want to show it,
If you're happy and you know it, clap your hands.

Continue the song with other actions:
stomp your feet, nod your head, turn around, etc.

Rock-a-Bye Baby

Rock-a-bye baby, on the treetops.
When the wind blows, the cradle will rock.
When the bough breaks, the cradle will fall,
And down will come baby, cradle and all.

Rain, Rain, Go Away

Rain, rain, go away;
Come again another day.
[Name] wants to play;
Come again another day.

I've Got the Joy

I've got the joy, joy, joy, joy,
Down in my heart,
Down in my heart,
Down in my heart;
I've got the joy, joy, joy, joy,
Down in my heart,
Down in my heart to stay.

Jesus Loves the Little Children

Jesus loves the little children,
All the children of the world.
All the children of the earth,
They are precious from their birth,
Jesus loves the little children of the world.

This Little Light of Mine

This little light of mine, I'm gonna let it shine.
This little light of mine, I'm gonna let it shine.
This little light of mine, I'm gonna let it shine,
Let it shine, let it shine, let it shine.

I'm in the Lord's Army

I may never march in the infantry,
Ride in the cavalry,
Shoot the artillery,
I may never shoot for the enemy,
But I'm in the Lord's army!
I'm in the Lord's army!
I'm in the Lord's army!
I may never march in the infantry,
Ride in the cavalry,
Shoot the artillery,
I may never shoot for the enemy,
But I'm in the Lord's army!

His Banner Over Me Is Love

His banner over me is love.
His banner over me is love.
He brought me into His banqueting house,
And His banner over me is love.
Is love! Is love!
His banner over me is love.
He brought me into His banqueting house,
And His banner over me is love.

The Wise Man Built His House Upon the Rock

The wise man built his house upon the rock.
The wise man built his house upon the rock.
The wise man built his house upon the rock.
And the rains came tumbling down.
The rains came down, and the floods came up.
The rains came down, and the floods came up.
The rains came down, and the floods came up.
And the house on the rock stood firm.

Twinkle, Twinkle, Little Star

Twinkle, twinkle, little star,
How I wonder what you are!
Up above the world so high,
Like a diamond in the sky.
Twinkle, twinkle, little star,
How I wonder what you are!

He's Got the Whole World in His Hands

He's got the whole world in His hands.
He's got the whole world in His hands.
He's got the whole world in His hands.
He's got the whole world in His hands.

Continue the song by listing people, animals, and things:
puppies and kitties, sunshine and rain,
grandma and grandpa, etc.

The B-I-B-L-E

The B-I-B-L-E,
Yes, that's the book for me;
I stand alone on the Word of God,
The B-I-B-L-E.

Jesus Loves Me

Jesus loves me, this I know,
For the Bible tells me so.
Little ones to Him belong;
They are weak, but He is strong.
Yes, Jesus loves me! Yes, Jesus loves me!
Yes, Jesus loves me! The Bible tells me so.

ABOUT THE AUTHOR

Allison Bemiss is a mom, educator, author, and speaker. She has worked to encourage critical and creative thinking in early childhood and elementary-age children for nearly 20 years, while serving as a teacher, interventionist, and education consultant. She currently leads workshops for early childhood and elementary educators in the areas of literacy, STEAM, and family engagement. You can also find her at the local library scouring the shelves with her sons for their next favorite reads or leading family storybook events. She lives in southern Kentucky with her husband, two boys, and one goldendoodle.